NATIONAL
GEOGRAPHIC
KiDS

Somebunny loves me

—sharing kindness with our animal friends—

Parry Gripp

NATIONAL GEOGRAPHIC
WASHINGTON, D.C.

Check out the song and music video at **natgeokids.com/somebunny**

IT's a book and a song!
Are you ready? Sing along.

Some**doggy**
is happy

to come home with me.
Together we play
and walk with a leash.

I give her fresh water
and good food to eat.
I hug her. I brush her
and give her a treat.

I teach Somedoggy
how to be her dog best.
I hold her paw
when we go to the vet.

She barks and she fetches
again and again.
Somedoggy loves me
and she's my best friend.

Somedoggy loves me!

Barkity bark.
Barkity bark, barkity bark!

Somefishy's so pretty.

She glitters and gleams.
She swims like a champ
on her fishy swim team.

I sprinkle her food in,
but only a touch.
To keep her tank clean
I don't put in too much.

Sometimes Somefishy
needs time to hide.
I just wait to see her
and don't tap on the side.

I check on Somefishy
after school every day.
Somefishy loves me
and I feel the same way.

Somefishy loves me!
Bloopity bloop.
Bloopity bloop, bloopity bloop!

Somekitty
curls up
and purrs on my knee.
I never pull his tail.
I pet him gently.

He bats at his toy.
He catches. He misses.
I give him a litter box
so he can do his business.

He always reminds me
when it's dinner time.
Somekitty loves me
and I'm so glad he's mine.

Somekitty loves me!

Meowity meow.
Meowity meow, meowity meow!

Sometortoise moves slowly
just as fast as he can.
I've made him a playground
with a pond and some sand.

I turn on a lamp
to warm his round back.
He nibbles on veggies
and worms for snacks.

I stroke his shell softly.
I don't force him to play.
Sometortoise loves me
and that makes my day.

Sometortoise loves me!
Boppity bop.
Boppity bop, boppity bop!

Somechickies
so fluffy,
peep-peeping away,
will grow up to become
Somechickens someday.

Strutting and pecking
they stretch skinny legs.
Clucking and squawking
they lay speckled eggs.

To keep them all safe
from raccoons and foxes
I've built a strong coop.
They nest in snug boxes.

Feathered heads
and prancing feet.
Somechickies love me
and I'm thrilled as can be.

Some chickies love me!

Peepity peep.
Peepity peep, peepity peep!

Somefuzzy

tosses

a toy with his teeth.
He likes his hair messy.
He likes his house neat.

Somefuzzy runs
on his wheel while I sleep.
I give him some seeds
to hide in his cheeks.

Somefuzzy explores.
He's brave, never bashful.
I've saved empty cartons
and made him a castle.

He's in after playtime.
I don't leave him out.
Somefuzzy loves me.
And we're pals—no doubt.

Somefuzzy loves me!

Squeakity Squeak.
Squeakity Squeak, Squeakity Squeak!

Somelizard
can climb up
her branch and sunbathe.
And like a small dragon,
she's cool in her cave.

When she needs a new outfit,
she just sheds her skin.
Somelizard loves me
through thick and thin.

Somelizard loves me!

Boopity boop.
Boopity boop, boopity boop!

Somepony

so splendid,

so strong and so tall.
I brush her all over
and clean out her stall.

Somepony, she whinnies
excited to know
I've brought her a carrot
and we're ready to go.

Riding along
she trots with delight.
The grass is her favorite.
She stops for a bite.

I braid her long mane
and give her back a good scratch.
Somepony loves me
and we're a perfect match.

Somepony loves me!
Clopity clop.
Clopity clop, clopity clop!

Some**bunny** is shy.

So I'm quiet and sweet.
He's softer than blankets.
Touch gently and see.

I give him big handfuls
of timothy hay.
He's silent but still likes
to dig, jump, and play.

Somebunny comes hopping
to say, "Snuggle me."
I love Somebunny, and
Somebunny loves me.

Some**bunny** loves **me!**

Hoppity hop.
Hoppity hop, hoppity hop!

Some pets are big,
Some pets are small.
Some swim and some fly.
Some leap and some crawl.

Whatever our pets need,
we make their days nice.

Show your pets love ♥
and they'll love you back twice!
♥

Somebunny loves me!

Hoppity hop.
Hoppity hop, hoppity hop!

I've always **loved** having a **pet share my home.**

I've got a bunny named Bruno, and he and a lot of my friends' pets are the inspirations behind so many of my songs. I'm amazed at how wonderfully intelligent, super athletic, or ridiculously cute pets can be! Every animal is unique, so I try to capture a creature's special personality when I write a story or a song or make a music video. It's also important to remember that every animal is unique when caring for one.

Maybe you have a pet, or are thinking of adopting one. Taking care of an animal is a big responsibility, but it's also one of the best experiences you can have.

It takes daily work to keep pets safe, clean, healthy, and happy. It also takes patience to train them and to handle them gently. Some pets need to walk and play every day. Some kinds of pets need baths or grooming— or even to have their teeth brushed! And like us, pets can get sick or hurt and need to go to the veterinarian (a doctor for animals).

All pets need clean water daily and healthy food. They need quiet and safe shelter—like a bed, a nest, a coop, a terrarium, or a tank—and these places need to be cleaned often. Ask a grown-up to help you with messes, and always wash your hands with warm water and soap.

Even if your pet doesn't communicate with you by barking or meowing, you can spend time with him and start to understand what he enjoys and needs. You can check out library books to learn more about your pet. Or talk to friends who have the same kind of pet you have and trade ideas about how to care for and enjoy them.

If you want to try to make your own pet music video, make sure your pet is happy and comfortable when you film her. I've found that the best pet videos are usually of an animal doing something they already know how to do or really like to do!

Pets can keep us company; be our friends; star in our photos, songs, and videos; and even become members of our families. Even though taking care of a pet is a big deal, it's totally worth it. I believe that by being friends with animals we can learn something about ourselves, and by treating animals with kindness and thoughtful care we can be better people. Take good care of your pets. While you're at it, read them this book; they might like it, too!

—*Parry Gripp*

For my mom, Anne, who taught me and so many other kids to love books. —P.G.

Since 1888, the National Geographic Society has funded more than 12,000 research, exploration, and preservation projects around the world. The Society receives funds from National Geographic Partners, LLC, funded in part by your purchase. A portion of the proceeds from this book supports this vital work. To learn more, visit natgeo.com/info.

NATIONAL GEOGRAPHIC and Yellow Border Design are trademarks of the National Geographic Society, used under license.

For more information, visit nationalgeographic.com, call 1-800-647-5463, or write to the following address:

National Geographic Partners
1145 17th Street N.W.
Washington, D.C. 20036-4688 U.S.A.

Visit us online at nationalgeographic.com/books

For librarians and teachers: ngchildrensbooks.org

More for kids from National Geographic: kids.nationalgeographic.com

For information about special discounts for bulk purchases, please contact National Geographic Books Special Sales: specialsales@natgeo.com

For rights or permissions inquiries, please contact National Geographic Books Subsidiary Rights: bookrights@natgeo.com

Designed by Julide Dengel

The publisher would like to thank the following people for making this book possible: Kate Hale, senior editor; Christina Ascani, associate photo editor; Julide Dengel, art director; Amy Novesky, text editor; Aylene Rhiger Gripp, consultant; Sally Abbey, managing editor; Joan Gossett, editorial production manager; Gus Tello, design production assistant.

Hardcover ISBN: 978-1-4263-2975-3
Reinforced library binding ISBN: 978-1-4263- 2976-0
Printed in Hong Kong
17/THK/1

PHOTO CREDITS:
COVER, Front: Charla Anne/Getty Images; Back (trade hardcover), Angela Lumsden/Stocksy; Back (Dust jacket and Library hardcover): (pony), Grigorita Ko/Shutterstock; (turtle), Northass/iStockPhoto; (dog), TheDogPhotographer/Getty Images; (cat), Kachalkina Veronika/Shutterstock; (chicks), PCHT/Shutterstock; (lizard), MilanEXPO/Getty Images; (hamster), Lusyaya/Getty Images; (fish), Arco Images/Alamy Stock Photo; 1, Purple Collar Pet Photography/Getty Images; 2, Mike Powell/Getty Images; 4–5, Sanjagrujic/Getty Images; 5 (LO), Grigorita Ko/Getty Image; 6 (LO), Liliya Kulianionak/Shutterstock; 6–7, SarahWolfePhotography/Getty Images; 8 (LO), Katrina Brown/Dreamstime; 8–9, Jose Luis Pelaez/Getty Images; 10, Oleh_Slobodeniuk/Getty Images; 11 (LO), Dmitry Kalinovsky/Shutterstock; 12 (LO), Dmitry Kalinovsky/Dreamstime; 13, Konrad Wothe/Minden Pictures; 14 (LO), Eric Isselee/Shutterstock; 14–15, Mint Images/Alamy Stock Photo; 16 (LO), Africa Studio/Shutterstock; 16-17, Rachel Weill/Getty Images; 18, Jasmin Sachtleben/EyeEm/Getty Images; 19 (LO), Igor Kovalchuk/Shutterstock; 20 (LO), Rudmer Zwerver/Shutterstock; 21, Angela Lumsden/Stocksy; 22 (LO), Robert Eastman/Shutterstock; 22–23, ApuuliWorld/Getty Images; 24 (LO), Callipso/Shutterstock; 24–25, Adie Bush/Getty Images; 26, Djem/Shutterstock; 27, Melanie Defazio/Stocksy; 28 (pony), Grigorita Ko/Shutterstock; 28 (turtle), Northass/iStockPhoto; 28 (dog), TheDogPhotographer/Getty Images; 28 (cat), Kachalkina Veronika/Shutterstock; 28 (chicks), PCHT/Shutterstock; 28 (lizard), MilanEXPO/Getty Images; 28 (hamster), Lusyaya/Getty Images; 28 (fish), Arco Images/Alamy Stock Photo; 29, Danielle D. Hughson/Getty Images; 30 (CTR), Dana Sherlock; 32, RTimages/Shutterstock